FAVORITE BASKETBALL TEAMS

Los Angeles Lakers

BY K. C. KELLEY

THE CHILD'S WORLD®
1980 Lookout Drive • Mankato, MN 56003-1705
800-599-READ • www.childsworld.com

ACKNOWLEDGMENTS
The Child's World®: Mary Berendes, Publishing Director
Shoreline Publishing Group, LLC: James Buckley, Jr.,
    Production Director
The Design Lab: Kathleen Petelinsek, Design;
    Gregory Lindholm, Page Production

PHOTOS
Cover and interior: AP/Wide World Photos

Published in the United States of America.
LIBRARY OF CONGRESS
CATALOGING-IN-PUBLICATION DATA
Kelley, K. C.
  Los Angeles Lakers / by K.C. Kelley.
      p. cm. — (Favorite basketball teams)
  Includes bibliographical references and index.
  ISBN 978-1-60253-309-7 (library bound : alk. paper)
  1. Los Angeles Lakers (Basketball team)—Juvenile literature.
  2. Basketball—California—Los Angeles—Juvenile literature.
  I. Title. II. Series.
  GV885.52.L65K45 2009
  796.323'640979494—dc22   2009009790

Table of Contents

Go, Lakers!

The Los Angeles Lakers play basketball in a city that makes movies. The Lakers put on an amazing show themselves! They have star players like the movies have stars. They win big games like movies win big awards. Like movies, the Lakers have millions of fans! Let's find out more about this awesome collection of shining (basketball!) stars.

Kobe Bryant is the leader of today's L.A. Lakers.

6

Here the Lakers celebrate winning the Western Conference in 2008.

Who Are the Lakers?

The Los Angeles Lakers play in the National Basketball Association (NBA). They are one of 30 teams in the NBA. The NBA includes the Eastern Conference and the Western Conference. The Lakers play in the Pacific Division of the Western Conference. The winner of the Eastern Conference plays the winner of the Western Conference in the **NBA Finals**. The Lakers have been the NBA champions 14 times—the second-most ever!

Where They Came From

The Lakers first played in 1948, when they were located in Minneapolis. They moved to Los Angeles in 1961. The first Lakers team was part of the Basketball Association of America (BAA). In 1949, that league joined with another to become the NBA. The Lakers got off to a very hot start. They were league champions five of their first six years! Then, from 1959 to 1970, they were great . . . just not great enough. They made it to the NBA Finals eight times—but lost every time to the Boston Celtics!

Wilt Chamberlain (13) was a Lakers star in the 1960s.

10

The Celtics (left) and the Lakers have long been cross-country rivals.

Who They Play

The Lakers play 82 games each season. That's a lot of basketball! They play every other NBA team at least once each season. They play teams in their division and conference more often. Since the 1960s, the Lakers have had a big **rivalry** with the Boston Celtics. Those two teams have often battled in the NBA Finals. The Lakers also play against another NBA team in Los Angeles, the Clippers.

Where They Play

The Lakers play their home games at the Staples Center. This large indoor arena holds about 19,000 people for Lakers games. The team moved into this home in 1999. The Staples Center is also home to the L.A. Clippers NBA team. It also is the home of the pro hockey L.A. Kings. Staples hosts rock concerts, skateboard shows, and lots of other events, too.

The Staples Center has become one of the NBA's most famous arenas.

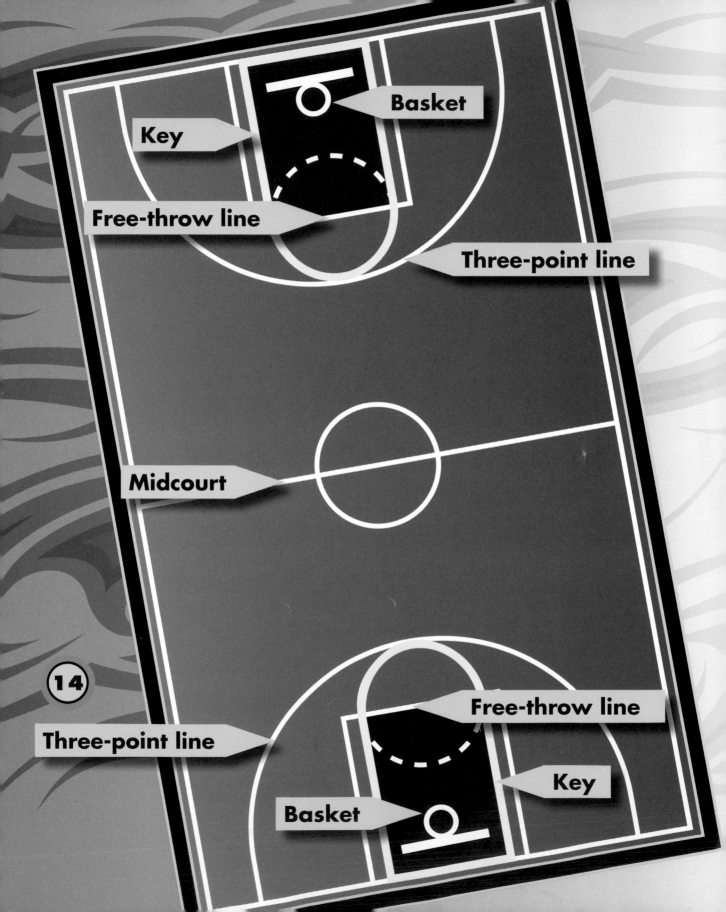

The Basketball Court

Basketball is played on a court made of wood. An NBA court is 94 feet (29 m) long. A painted line shows the middle of the court. Other lines lay out the free-throw area. The space below each basket is known as the "key." The baskets at each end are 10 feet (3 m) off the ground. The metal rims of the baskets stick out over the court. Nylon nets hang from the rims.

Big Days!

The Los Angeles Lakers have had many great moments in their long history. Here are three of the greatest:

1949: The Lakers won their first NBA championship. It was the start of a streak of five titles in six years.

1972: During the season, the team won a record 33 games in a row. They went on to win their first NBA title since 1954.

2009: The Lakers won their fifteenth NBA title! Coach Phil Jackson set an NBA record by winning his tenth title (he won six of them while coaching the Chicago Bulls).

This 2002 NBA championship was the Lakers' third in a row.

18

Vlade Divac (center) and other Lakers lost a lot of games in 2005.

Tough Days!

The Lakers can't win all their games. Some games or seasons don't turn out well. The players keep trying to play their best, though! Here are some of the toughest seasons in Lakers history:

1958: The Lakers were the NBA champs in 1954. Just a few years later, they won only 19 and lost 53.

2005: The Lakers missed the **playoffs.** Other than this year and 1994, they made them every year from 1977 to 2004!

2008: The Lakers battled their old rivals, the Celtics, in the NBA Finals. The Celtics walloped the Lakers 131–92 in the final game to capture the title.

Meet the Fans

Lakers games are filled with stars. They're not just on the court, either! Many movie stars and music heroes go to Lakers games. They get to sit very close to the court. They meet the players and then cheer for them! Many Lakers fans watch the movie and music stars as much as they watch the Lakers players.

21

Confetti flew during the Lakers' 2001 victory party.

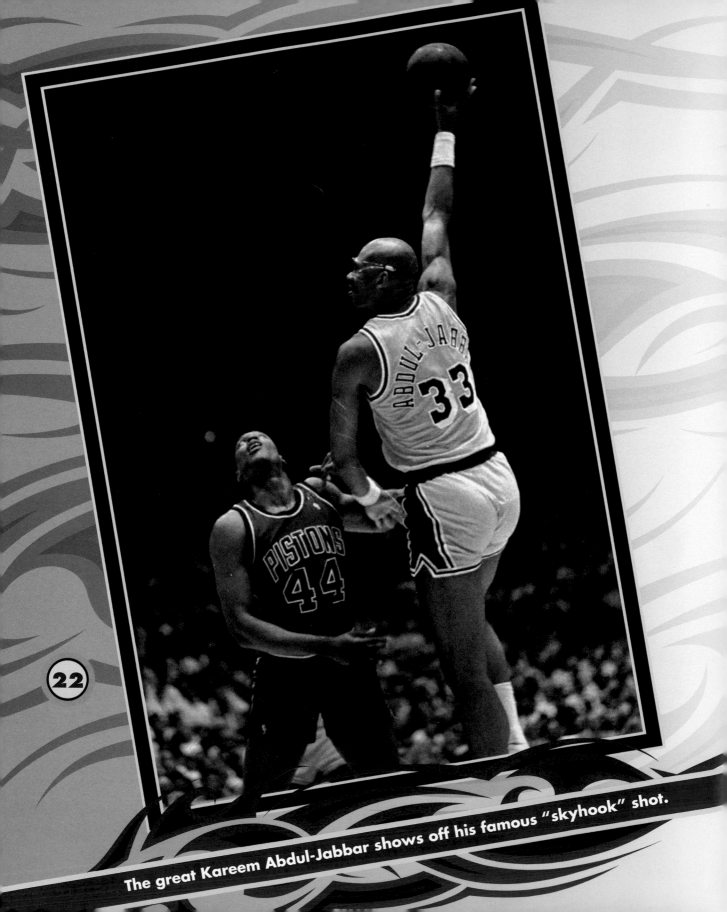

The great Kareem Abdul-Jabbar shows off his famous "skyhook" shot.

Heroes Then...

The Lakers have had superstars at every position–including **center**. George Mikan was the NBA's first great center. He helped the Lakers win their first five NBA titles. Another center, Wilt Chamberlain, was one of the highest-scoring players ever. Kareem Abdul-Jabbar played first with the Milwaukee Bucks but joined the Lakers in 1975. He scored more points than anyone else in NBA history! Another center, Shaquille O'Neal, was almost impossible to stop. Elgin Baylor and James Worthy were great **forwards**. **Guard** Jerry West led the Lakers in the 1960s. He had an awesome shooting touch. Magic Johnson was a guard, but he could play any position. His great smile teamed with his great play to make him a hero.

Heroes Now...

Kobe Bryant is perhaps the best player in the NBA. He once scored 81 points in a game! He can make amazing leaps and **slam dunks**. He also can make a shot from just about anywhere. Kobe always comes through when his team really needs him. He is helped by forward Pau Gasol, who is from Spain. Young Andrew Bynum follows in the Lakers' long line of great centers.

25

Pau Gasol has great dribbling skills for such a tall player.

Gearing Up

Los Angeles Lakers players wear a uniform and special basketball sneakers. Some wear other pads to protect themselves. Check out this picture of Lamar Odom and learn about what NBA players wear.

The Basketball

NBA basketballs are made of leather. Several pieces are held together with rubber edges. Inside the leather ball is a hollow ball of rubber. This is filled with air. The leather is covered with little bumps called "pebbles." The pebbles help players get a good grip on the ball. The basketball used in the Women's National Basketball Association (WNBA) is slightly smaller than the men's basketball.

Wristband

Jersey

Shorts

Knee brace

Elbow brace

Socks

Basketball shoes

27

Lamar Odom is a high-flying Lakers player.

Sports Stats

Note: All numbers shown are through the 2008–2009 season.

HIGH SCORERS

These players have scored the most points for the Lakers.

PLAYER	POINTS
Jerry West	25,192
Kareem Abdul-Jabbar	24,176

HELPING HAND

Here are the Lakers' all-time leaders in **assists**.

PLAYER	ASSISTS
Magic Johnson	10,141
Jerry West	6,238

CLEANING THE BOARDS

Rebounds are a big part of the game. Here are the Lakers' best rebounders.

PLAYER	REBOUNDS
Elgin Baylor	11,463
Kareem Abdul-Jabbar	10,279

MOST THREE-POINT SHOTS MADE

Shots taken from behind a line about 23 feet (7 m) from the basket are worth three points. Here are the Lakers' best at these long-distance shots.

PLAYER	THREE-POINT SHOTS
Kobe Bryant	1,204
Nick Van Exel	750

COACH

Who coached the Lakers to the most wins?

Pat Riley, 533

Glossary

assists passes to teammates that lead directly to making baskets

center a player (usually the tallest on the team) who plays close to the basket

forward one of two tall players who rebound and score near the basket

guard one of two players who set up plays, pass to teammates closer to the basket, and shoot from farther away

NBA Finals the seven-game NBA championship series, in which the champion must win four games

playoffs a series of games between 16 teams that decide which two teams will play in the NBA Finals

rebounds missed shots that bounce off the backboard or rim and are often grabbed by another player

rivalry an ongoing competition between teams that play each other often, over a long time

slam dunks shots made by stuffing the basketball ball in the hoop

Find Out More

Books

Christopher, Matt. *Greatest Moments in Basketball History*. New York: Little, Brown, 2009.

Craats, Rennay. *Basketball*. Toronto: Weigl Publishers, 2008.

Hareas, John. *Eyewitness Basketball*. New York: DK, 2005.

Kirkpatrick, Rob. *Kobe Bryant*. New York: Rosen Publishing, 2008.

McRae, Sloane. *The Los Angeles Lakers*. New York: PowerKids Press, 2009.

Web Sites

Visit our Web page for links about the Los Angeles Lakers and other NBA teams:

childsworld.com/links

Note to Parents, Teachers, and Librarians: We routinely verify our Web links to make sure they are safe, active sites—so encourage your readers to check them out!

Index

K. C. KELLEY

K. C. Kelley has written dozens of books on basketball, football, baseball, and other sports for young readers. K. C. used to work for NFL Publishing and has covered several Super Bowls. He likes to watch any basketball game, but the Los Angeles Lakers are his favorite team.